MAINTAIN YOUR STRONG MINDSETS!

Birister Sharma

Dedicated to my loving wife....

Pallabi Devi Sharma

I surrendered to you, O my Lord......

"Om Namah Shivaya"

Table of Contents

One Word

If you know your mindset, you'll know how to win everything in your life.

If you know your mindset, nobody can defeat you.

If you know your mindset, you'll know your strengths.

If you know your mindset, you can change your life.

If you know your mindset, you can change your world.

If you know your mindset, you can change everything in your life.

It's only your mindset that decides your destiny.

It's only your mindset that decides your success and glory.

You can win everything in your life.

You can achieve everything in your life.

If you've a positive mindset, you'll become positive.

If you've a negative mindset, you'll become negative.

If you've a strong mindset, you'll become strong.

If you've a weak mindset, you'll become weak.

Nobody can change your mindset.

Only you can change your mindset.

Change your mindset and change your life.

~***~

Chapter 1

Wait for the right moment

Nothing happens before time.

Nothing happens after time.

Everything happens at the right time.

A plant always bears flowers and fruits at the right time or at the right season.

A farmer always waits for the right season to sow the seeds of the food grains in his field.

The right things will always happen at the right time.

This is the universal law.

Nobody can deny it.

If the bad things are happening in your life at the moment, it means your good things are yet to come.

You've to wait for the right moment.

Give time to yourself.

Nobody can steal your glorious moment of your life.

Don't worry.

Just wait for the right moment.

Your D-day will definitely come.

If the bad things are happening in your life at the moment, it means your good things are yet to come.

Once upon a time, in a small village nestled among the rolling hills, there lived a young girl named Lily. She was known in the village for her patience and perseverance, and she had a dream that burned brightly in her heart- to become a skilled archer.

Ever since she was a child, Lily had been fascinated by the art of archery. She would often watch the local archers practicing their skills with awe, and dreamt of the day when she could join their ranks. However, she knew that she was too young and inexperienced to take up a bow and arrow just yet.

Despite her eagerness, Lily understood the importance of waiting for the right moment. She knew that rushing into things without proper preparation could lead to failure. So, she decided to be patient and wait for the right time to pursue her passion.

As the years passed, Lily grew into a young woman, but her determination to become an archer never wavered. She spent her days observing the archers in the village, learning from their techniques and practicing her skills with makeshift bows and arrows she crafted herself. She also sought the guidance of the village elder, who was a master archer himself.

One day, a renowned archery tournament was announced in the nearby city. It was a prestigious event, and the winner would receive a grand prize and earn a chance to train with the kingdom's elite archers. Lily's heart swelled with excitement, and she longed to participate in the tournament.

However, she knew that she was not yet ready. Her arrows didn't fly as straight as wanted them to, and her aim was not as precise as it needed to be. She could have easily rushed into entering the tournament, but she remembered her vows to wait for the right moment.

So, with unwavering determination, Lily focused on honing her skills. She practiced tirelessly, putting in countless hours of hard work and dedication. She sought advice from the village elder, who provided her with invaluable guidance and mentorship.

As the tournament drew nearer, Lily's progress was evident. Her arrows found their mark more accurately, and her shots were getting more powerful. She was growing in confidence, but she still knew that she had more to learn.

Finally, the day of the tournament arrived. Lily watched as archers from all over the kingdom gathered to compete. Her heart yearned to join them, but she took a deep breath and reminded herself to wait for the right moment.

She continued to practice and refine her skills, observing the techniques of other skilled archers and learning from them. She remained patient, waiting for the right opportunity to arise.

On the final day of the tournament, as the sun was setting and tension filled the air, Lily finally felt ready. She approached the registration desk with a calm and determined demeanor, and she entered her name into the competition.

The tournament commenced, and Lily gave it her all. She shot arrow after arrow, hitting her targets with precision and speed. The competition was fierce, but she remained focused and determined, using all the skills she had honed over the years.

In the end, Lily emerged as one of the finalist, and she faced off against a skilled archer from a distant kingdom. The final round was intense, with both archers showcasing their talents. But in the end, it was Lily's patience, perseverance, and skill that paid off.

With her final arrow, she hit the bull's-eye, winning the tournament and earning the grand prize. The crowd erupted into applause as she stood on the podium, her heart swelling with joy and pride.

As she stood there, basking in her victory, Lily realized that her journey had been about more than just winning a tournament. It had been a lesson in patience, perseverance, and the importance.

~***~

How can you maintain your strong mindset?

- Keep your dream alive.

- Persevere.

- Have patience.

- Be passionate about whatever you do in your life.

- Gain experience at your expertise

- Learn to wait.

- Don't rush to do anything.

- Prepare yourself every day.

- Be determined.

- Polish your own talents and skills.

- Focus on your goal.

- Be confident.

- Believe in yourself.

~***~

"Optimism is the faith that leads to achievement. Nothing can be done without hope and confidence."

---Helen Keller

Chapter 2

Be optimistic

Be optimistic in your life.

No matter whatever happens in your life whether good or bad, keep your hope high and alive.

Always remember that if there is nothing left in your life, then there is always hope.

Keep the rays of hope in your life.

Always try to see the silver lining in the dark clouds.

If you're optimistic, you'll never break down in your life.

You'll always bounce back after every downfall.

Your good time will definitely come.

Just wait and see, and do your work.

Don't try to look back.

Move ahead and never turn back.

Accept your setbacks, and learn from it.

Improve yourself every day.

Success and failure are temporary in your life.

Happiness and sorrow are short-lived in your life.

If you're optimistic, you can face every failure and every sorrow like your success and happiness.

You can handle every situation with ease.

Always remember that if there is nothing left in your life, then there is always hope.

Once upon a time, in a quaint little village nestled in the rolling hills, there lived a young girl named Payal. Payal was known far and wide for her unwavering optimism. She had a unique ability to see the bright side of every situation, no matter how challenging or bleak it may seem.

Payal's positivity was contagious, and she was loved by everyone in the village. She had a cheerful disposition and a warm smile that could brighten even the cloudiest of days. She was always willing to lend a helping hand to those in need, and her optimism was a guiding light for those around her.

One day, a terrible drought struck the village. The fields turned brown, and the rivers dried up. The villagers were devastated as their crops withered and their livestock suffered. Many of them lost hope and were filled with despair.

But not Payal. She remained optimistic and hopeful, despite the dire circumstances. She encouraged her fellow villagers to stay positive and not give up. She rallied them to come together as a community and find solutions to tackle the drought.

Payal used her creativity and resourcefulness to come up with innovative ideas. She organized water-saving workshops, taught the villagers about drought-resistant crops, and helped them implement sustainable farming practices. She also organized community gatherings to boost morale and lift spirits during this challenging time.

Her unwavering optimism and tireless efforts inspired the villagers to follow her lead. They worked together, digging wells, collecting rainwater, and using water efficiently. They supported each other and remained hopeful, even when things seemed tough.

Months passed, and the drought persisted, but Payal's optimism never wavered. She kept spreading positivity, and her resilience was a beacon of hope for the villager. Her efforts started to bear fruit, and gradually, the situation began to improve.

One day, as the villagers were gathered around a newly dug well, celebrating their success, raindrops started falling from the sky. The long-awaited rain had finally arrived, breaking the drought. The villagers rejoiced, and Payal's heart swelled with joy.

With the arrival of rain, the fields turned green, and the rivers flowed again. The village flourished once more, and the villagers were filled with gratitude for Payal's unwavering optimism and leadership during the challenging times.

Years passed, and Payal grew older, but her optimism remained unchanged. She continued to spread positivity and inspire those around her. Her reputation as the village's eternal optimist spread beyond the village, and she became known as a beacon of hope in the entire region.

Payal's unwavering optimism had a ripple effect, and her village had transformed into a thriving and closely-knit community. Her legacy lived on, and her positive outlook had touched the lives of countless people.

As she sat on her porch, watching the sunset one day, Payal felt grateful for the life she had lived. She realized that her optimism had not only helped her overcome challenges but had also made a positive impact on the lives of others. She smiled, knowing that her optimism had been her greatest strength and had made the world a better place.

And so, the story of Payal, the eternal optimist, continued to inspire generations to come, reminding everyone that no matter how dark the clouds may seem, a positive outlook and unwavering optimism can light up even the darkest of days.

How can you maintain your strong mindset?

- Keep your unwavering optimism.

- See the bright side of every situation.

- Keep your positive outlook.

- Be cheerful.

- Keep your broad smile on your face.

- Help yourself and help others in their needs.

- Don't lose your hope.

- Encourage yourself.

- Find your solution in every problem.

- Don't worry or panic in the difficult situation.

- Be creative in your every approach.

- Boost up your moral every day.

~***~

"Make a game of finding something positive in every situation. Ninety-five percent of your emotions are determined by how you interpret events to yourself."

---Brain Tracy

Chapter 3

Be positive in every situation

Be positive in every situation.

You'll never change the situation in your life, but you can change yourself.

If you change yourself according to the situation, you can handle or manage every situation in your life.

If you keep yourself positive in every situation, every situation will turn in your favor.

If you keep yourself positive in every situation, every situation will become your closed friend.

Make friends with the situation.

You'll never move against the situation.

But you can move with the situation.

If you keep yourself positive, you can motivate yourself.

If you keep yourself positive, you can guide yourself.

If you keep yourself positive, you can see possibilities in every impossible situation.

You'll never become distressed and upset in your life.

You can live in every situation.

You can solve your every problem.

You can find new ways and directions in every tough situation.

You'll become the master of every situation.

But, if you're negative, you'll always become distressed and upset even the situation is in your favor.

If you change yourself according to the situation, you can handle or manage every situation in your life.

~***~

Anecdote:

In a bustling city, there lived a young woman named Shanti. Shanti was known for her unshakable positivity and her ability to find the silver lining in every situation. She had a bright smile that could light up a room and a heart full of optimism that never wavered, no matter what challenges came her way.

Shanti worked as a nurse in a busy hospital. Her days were filled with caring for patients, comforting families, and navigating the ups and downs of the healthcare profession. She faced long hours, challenging cases, and sometimes even heartbreaking situations, but she always maintained a positive attitude.

One day, while on her way to work, Shanti's car broke down. She was already running late and felt her initial frustration rising. However, instead of dwelling on the inconvenience, Shanti took a deep breath and decided to make the most of the situation. She called for help, then took a leisurely walk to the hospital, enjoying the fresh air and taking in the sights and sounds of the city along the way.

As Shanti arrived at the hospital, she learned that it was an exceptionally busy day. There was a shortage of staff due to unforeseen circumstances, and the emergency room was flooded with patients. Despite the chaos, Shanti remained calm and focused on providing the best care possible to her patients. She used her positivity to lift the spirits of her colleagues and motivate them to work together as a team.

Throughout the day, Shanti encountered patients who were scared, anxious, and in pain. But she used her positive outlook to offer words of comfort, encouragement, and support. She held the hand of an elderly patient, listened patiently to a young child's fears, and offered a shoulder to cry on for a grieving family.

Her positive attitude not only brought comfort to her patients but also had a profound impact on her colleagues. Her unwavering optimism and can-do attitude inspired them to keep pushing forward despite the challenges they faced.

As the day turned into night, Shanti's shift finally ended. She felt physically exhausted but emotionally fulfilled. She knew that her positivity had made a difference in the lives of her patients and her colleagues.

On her way back, Shanti reflected on her day. She realized that being positive in every situation wasn't always easy, but it was a choice she consciously made. She understood that positivity wasn't about denying the existence of challenges or difficulties, but rather about choosing to approach them with a mindset of resilience, hope and determination.

Shanti's positive outlook didn't end at work. She carried it with her in all aspects of her life. She found joy in simple pleasures, appreciated the beauty of everyday moments, and remained grateful for the blessings in her life.

Over time, Shanti's positivity became contagious. Her friends sought her advice during their tough times, her family admired her unwavering optimism, and her colleagues looked up to her as a role model. She became known as the person who could always find the bright side of any situation and offer words of encouragement and support.

As the years passed, Shanti continued to spread positivity wherever she went. She faced challenges and setbacks in her own life, but her positive attitude never wavered. She inspired countless people to approach life with a positive mindset, and her impact was felt far and wide.

Shanti's unwavering positivity not only enriched her own life but also touched the lives of others. She learned that being positive in every situation wasn't just about seeing the glass half full, but about finding the opportunities for growth, learning, and connection, even in the midst of challenges. Shanti's story became a beacon of inspiration, a reminder to everyone that a positive outlook can make a real difference in the world, one situation at a time.

How can you maintain your strong mindset?

- Be positive.

- Find the silver lining in every situation of your life.

- Try to smile.

- Keep your mind and heart open to everything.

- Maintain balance in your life.

- Handle every situation with a cool and calm mind.

- Do your best.

- Learn the new things every day.

- Face every challenge bravely.

- Discover joy in simple pleasures.

- Appreciate the beauty of every moment.

- Be grateful for the blessings of life.

- Find opportunities for your growth.

26

"Never stop learning, because life never stops teaching."

---Anonymous

Chapter 4

Never stop your learning

Learn from every situation of your life.

Learn from every person you meet in your life.

Learn from your friends.

Even learn from your enemies.

Learn from your elders.

Learn from your younger ones.

Even learn from children.

But, never hesitate to learn.

Never feel ashamed to learn.

Every event in your life whether good or bad, it will always teach you something meaningful.

You've to learn from it.

You can learn more from your failures rather than from your successes.

You can learn more from your hardships rather than from your gala days.

Learning is a never ending process.

Never allow to dry up your learning skills.

The more you learn, the more you'll grow in your life; and the more you grow in your life, the more you'll enrich your life.

If you want to nurture your life, then you've to learn every moment and every day.

Every event in your life whether good or bad, it will always teach you something meaningful.

Anecdote:

Once upon a time, in a quaint village nestled amidst rolling hills, there lived a young girl named Anita. Anita was a curious child who loved to learn. She spent her days exploring the world around her, asking questions, and seeking knowledge wherever she could find it.

Anita's thirst for learning was insatiable. She would often be found with her nose buried in books borrowed from the village library or engaged in deep conversations with the elders in the village, eager to learn from their wisdom and experience. Her parents were supportive of her inquisitive nature and encouraged her to never stop learning.

As she grew older, Anita's passion for learning only grew stronger. She longed to know more about the world beyond her village, and she dreamt of embarking on grand adventures to quench her thirst for knowledge. One day, an opportunity presented itself when a traveling scholar visited the village. He was on a quest to gather information about different cultures and traditions, and he needed an apprentice to accompany him on his journey.

Anita, fueled by her curiosity and passion for learning, eagerly volunteered to join the scholar. Her parents, though sad to see her go, supported her decision, knowing that she was meant for great things. With her bag packed and heart full of excitement, Anita bid farewell to her family and friends and set off on her grand adventure with the scholar.

The journey was not always easy. Anita faced many challenges along the way, from harsh weather to dangerous encounters with animals. But she never wavered in her determination to learn. She soaked up knowledge like a sponge, eagerly absorbing everything she could from the scholar and the people they met on their travels.

They visited ancient libraries, studied with wise sages, and learned about different cultures, languages, and traditions. Anita's mind expanded with each new experience, and her heart swelled with gratitude for the opportunity to learn and grow.

One day, while exploring a dense forest in a foreign land, Anita stumbled upon a hidden cave. Intrigued, she ventured inside and discovered an ancient scroll containing a secret code. She was determined to decipher it, as it seemed to hold a treasure trove of knowledge.

With unwavering determination, Anita spent days and nights decoding the intricate puzzle. She poured over ancient texts, consulted with experts, and experimented with different methods until; finally, she cracked the code. It revealed a hidden chamber within the cave, filled with rare books and scrolls containing ancient knowledge lost to time.

Overwhelmed with joy, Anita delved into the treasure trove knowledge, hungrily devouring the ancient texts. She discovered forgotten wisdom, ancient philosophies, and untold stories of civilizations long gone. She learned about the stars, the secrets of the universe, and the mysteries of life.

Years passed, and Anita grew into a wise and learned scholar herself. She traveled far and wide, sharing her knowledge and wisdom with others, and inspiring them to never stop learning. She taught in prestigious institutions, mentored young minds, and made significant contributions to the fields of history, philosophy, and science.

One day, while sitting under a starry sky, Anita reflected on her incredible journey. She realized that her thirst for knowledge was unquenchable, and she would continue to learn and grow until her last breath. She understood that learning was a lifelong pursuit, and it had brought her immeasurable joy, fulfillment, and meaning in her life.

With a grateful heart, Anita decided to return to her village, where she was warmly welcomed as a revered scholar. She shared her stories and experiences, and her wisdom was treasured by all. She continued to inspire young minds to embrace the joy of learning and to never stop seeking knowledge.

And so, Anita's legacy lived on, as generations.

How can you maintain your strong mindset?

- Always be curious to learn.

- Explore the things around you.

- Keep asking questions to yourself and others.

- Seek knowledge wherever you could find it.

- Keep the thirst of your learning.

- Keep your burning passion alive.

- Utilize your precious time for learning new skills and art.

- Gain the experiences of life.

"You are never too old to set another goal or to dream a new dream."

---C. S. Lewis

Chapter 5

Never forget your life's goal

Never forget your life's goal.

Stand still until you will not achieve your life's goal.

Keep your life's goal the top most priority.

Wherever you go; wherever you live; and whatever you do in your life, don't forget your life's goal.

A man without goal is like a bird without wings.

Always clear your life's goal before you move on in your life.

Whatever you want to achieve in your life; clear your goal.

Whatever you want to earn in your life; clear your goal.

Whatever you want to do in your life; clear your goal.

Whatever you want to accomplish in your life; clear your goal.

If you can't clear your life's goal, you'll never reach anywhere in your life.

You'll wander hither and thither.

You'll become like a nomad.

Your life will become meaningless and purposeless.

You'll become like an animal.

You can only define your life with your goal.

No goal, no life, and nothing.

Wherever you go; wherever you live; and whatever you do in your life, don't forget your life's goal.

~***~

In a bustling city, amidst the skyscrapers and the rush of everyday life, there lived a young man named Rahul. From a young age, Rahul had a passion for art. He would spend hours doodling, sketching, and painting, lost in his won world of creativity. His dream was to become a renowned artist and share his unique perspective with the world.

As Rahul grew older, the responsibilities of adulthood began to pile up. He got a job, paid bills, and navigated the complexities of everyday life. He found himself caught in the hustle and bustle of the city, and his dreams of becoming an artist began to fade into the background.

One day, while cleaning his apartment, Rahul stumbled upon an old box filled with his art supplies from his childhood. Memories of his passion for art came flooding back, and he realized that he had lost sight of his life's goal in the chaos of his busy life. He felt a deep sense of longing, and he knew that he needed to reconnect with his artistic aspirations.

With renewed determination, Rahul made a promise to himself to never forget his life's goal again. He decided to make time for his art amidst his busy schedule, no matter how challenging it might be. He set up a small studio in his apartment, dusted off his art supplies, and began creating with renewed zeal.

At first, it wasn't easy; Rahul faced many obstacles, including self-doubt and lack of time. But his persevered, fueled by his passion for art and the memory of his childhood dreams. He painted during his lunch breaks, sketched during his commute, and stayed up late into the night perfecting his craft.

As he poured his heart and soul into his artwork, Rahul's talent began to shine. He experimented with different styles, techniques, and mediums, constantly pushing the boundaries of his creativity. He shared his artwork on social media and started participating in local art shows, slowly building a following of admirers who were captivated by his unique perspective.

Despite the challenges, Rahul remained steadfast in his pursuit of his life's goal. He made sacrifices, prioritized his passion for art, and never lost sight of his dreams. His determination and perseverance paid off, and he began receiving recognition for his work. He was invited to showcase his art in galleries, and his pieces started selling at impressive prices.

As his artistic career flourished, Rahul felt a deep sense of fulfillment and joy. He realized that he had rediscovered his purpose in life and was living true to his authentic self. He was grateful for the journey that had brought him back to his life's goal and for the unwavering support of his friends and family who had believed in him all along.

Years passed, and Rahul became a renowned artist, known for his unique style and artistic vision. He traveled the world, showcasing his artwork in prestigious galleries and connecting with fellow artists and art enthusiasts from different cultures and backgrounds. He never forgot the lesson he had learned- to never lose sight of his life's goal and to always prioritize his passion for art.

In the twilight of his career, Rahul looked back with pride and contentment. He had achieved his childhood dream and had made a meaningful impact on the world through his art. He was grateful for the unwavering pursuit if his life's goal and the profound sense of purpose it had given him.

As Rahul put down his paintbrush for the last time, he smiled, knowing that he had lived a life true to himself, and his legacy as an artist would continue to inspire others for generations to come. He hoped that his story would serve as a reminder to never forget one's life's goal and to pursue it with unwavering determination, no matter the challenging along the way.

How can you maintain your strong mindset?

- Love your own passion.

- Dream big.

- Don't allow your dreams to fade away.

- Persevere to transform your dreams into realities.

- Don't lose the sight of your life's goal.

- Realize and re-discover yourself.

- Connect with your life's aspirations.

- Renew your aims and objectives of life.

- Adjust and manage your time properly for your goal, even in your busy schedule.

- Give up your self-doubt.

- Push the boundaries of your limitations.

• Remain steadfast in your pursuit of your life's goal.

• Be ready to sacrifice (e.g. sacrifice your laziness, comfort, instant gratification, and bad habits).

• Prioritize your passion for your goal.

• Discover the purpose your life.

• Live true to yourself.

~***~

"Life is short. Focus on what really matters most; you should change your priorities over time."

---Roy T. Bennett

Chapter 6

Identify your topmost priority

What is your topmost priority in your life?

Figure out your topmost priority in your life.

Identify your topmost priority in your life.

Once you can identify your topmost priority in your life, then just go for it, and do it until you wouldn't accomplish it.

If your topmost priority is your work, then just do your work.

Don't do anything.

If your topmost priority is your family, then just do your duty towards your family.

Don't do anything.

If your topmost priority is your career, then just concentrate on your career.

Don't do anything.

If you know your topmost priority of your life, then nobody can stop you to accomplish your desire goal.

Discard which is not important for you.

Discover which thing is significant for you and which thing is insignificant for you.

If you do important things in your life, you'll become an important person in your life.

On the other hand, if you do unimportant things in your life, you'll become an unimportant person in your life.

If you know your topmost priority of your life, then nobody can stop you to accomplish your desire goal.

Aruna's topmost priority in life was her family. She had always been a doting mother to her three children, Anil, Babu, and Chandra, and a loving wife to her husband, Menak. She would go to any length to ensure their well-being and happiness.

One fateful day, Aruna received devastating news. Menak, her beloved husband, was diagnosed with a terminal illness. The doctors informed her that he had limited time left, and the news shattered Aruna's world. She was determined to make the most of the time they had left together and make Menak's final days as meaningful and memorable as possible.

Aruna rallied her children, and they came together as a family like never before. They spent precious moments with Menak, creating cherished memories that would last a lifetime. They took family trips, cooked favorite meals, and shared stories and laughter. Aruna poured all her energy into caring for Menak, making sure he was comfortable and surrounded by love.

As Menak's health declined, Aruna remained unwavering in her love and care for him. She put her own needs and desires aside, devoting herself entirely to her husband and children. She juggled the responsibilities of caring for Menak, managing the household, and supporting her children emotionally with grace and determination.

Throughout the difficult journey, Aruna's unwavering love and selflessness inspired those around her. Her children learned the true meaning of compassion, empathy, and sacrifice. They saw their mother's strength and resilience, and it left an indelible mark on their hearts.

In Menak's final moments, surrounded by Aruna and their children, he expressed his profound gratitude for Aruna's unwavering love. He thanked her for being his rock, his confidence, and his guiding light during his darkest days. He told her that he was at peace knowing that his family would be in her capable hands after he was gone.

After Menak passed away, Aruna grieved deeply, but she remained resolute in her commitment to her family. She continued to prioritize her children's well-being and happiness, guiding them through their grief and helping them navigate the challenges that life threw at them.

Years passed, and Aruna's children grew into successful and compassionate individuals, carrying forward the lessons of love and selflessness that their mother had taught them. Aruna watched with pride as they pursued their dreams and made a positive impact on the world.

As Aruna looked back on her life, she realized that her unwavering love for her family had been her topmost priority, and it had brought her immeasurable joy and fulfillment. Her heart swelled with love and pride as she saw her children thriving, and she knew that her legacy of love would continue for generations to come.

In the end, Aruna's unwavering love had left an enduring mark on her family, and her selflessness had made a profound difference in their lives. Her story became a testament to the power of unconditional love and the enduring bond of family. Aruna's topmost priority had shaped her life and the lives of her loved ones, and her legacy of love lived on forever.

How can you maintain your strong mindset?

- Love your beloved ones.

- You must know your topmost priority.

- Be ready to accept anything in your life.

- Make every moment meaningful and memorable.

- Don't break down, but bounce back.

- Surround yourself with your love ones.

- Devote yourself in your work.

- Follow your own duty and responsibility.

- Manage yourself as well as manage your dear ones.

- Support your family members emotionally, morally and financially.

- Learn the true meaning of compassion, empathy and sacrifice.

• Never forget to express your gratitude.

• Remain resolute to your own commitment towards your family as well as towards your work.

• Prioritize your own well-being and happiness as well as to your love ones.

• Guide yourself as well as your fellow mates.

• Help yourself to navigate the challenges of your life.

~***~

"The best things in life come in threes, like friends, dreams, and memories."

---Mencius

Chapter 7

Always select the best things in your life

Always select the best things in your life.

You have every right to select the best things for yourself.

Never compromise yourself while making the best selection in your life.

If you select good things today, you'll always get good things tomorrow.

If you select better things today, you'll always get better things tomorrow.

If you select the best things today, you'll always get the best things tomorrow.

But if you select bad things today, you'll always get the bad things tomorrow.

Your selection decides your future.

If you sow the best quality of seeds today, you'll reap the best fruits in the near future.

On the other hand, if you sow the poor quality of seeds today, you'll reap the same quality of fruits in the near future.

Before you select anything, observe, think, analyze and judge deeply, then go for the best selection.

Don't make haste when you select anything.

Don't select anything on the basis of its quantities.

Always select everything on the basis of its qualities.

Never compromise yourself while making the best selection in your life.

Savi was a young woman with a strong belief in always selecting the best things in life. She had been taught by her parents to strive for excellence and to never settle for mediocrity. From her academics to her hobbies, Savi always gave her best and aimed for the top.

Savi's pursuit of excellence was evident in her academic achievements. She excelled in school, consistently earning top grades and receiving accolades for her exceptional performance. She was known for her diligence, determination, and unwavering commitment to excellence.

In addition to her academics, Savi had a passion for music. She had been playing the piano since she was a child and had won several competitions at a young age. She practiced rigorously, honing her skills and always pushing herself to improve. Her dedication to her craft paid off, and she was recognized as one of the best pianists in her city.

Despite her busy schedule, Savi also made time for her family and friends. She nurtured meaningful relationships and surrounded herself with people who shared her values and aspirations. She believed that having a supportive network of loved ones was crucial in her pursuit of excellence, and she valued their encouragement and motivation.

As Savi grew older, she faced challenges and setbacks, as everyone does. However, she never lost sight of her belief in selecting the best things in life. When faced with obstacles, she saw them as opportunities to learn and grow, rather than reasons to settle for less. She persevered, maintaining her unwavering commitment to excellence in all areas of her life.

Savi's pursuit of excellence brought her many opportunities. She was offered scholarships to prestigious universities, and she chose to study at one of the best institutions in her field of interest. She continued to excel academically and was involved in various extracurricular activities, further honing her skills and broadening her horizons.

After graduating with top honors, Savi embarked on her professional career. She applied the same principles of excellence that she had followed throughout her life, and she quickly rose through the ranks in her field. Her dedication and exceptional performance earned her recognition and respect from her peers and superiors.

Despite her achievements, Savi remained grounded and humble. She continued to pursuit excellence in her personal life as well, maintaining meaningful relationships and engaging in activities that brought her joy and fulfillment. She found a balance between her professional success and personal well-being, recognizing that both were important aspects of a fulfilling life.

As Savi reflected on her journey, she realized that her unwavering commitment to selecting the best things in life had shaped her into the person she was today. She was grateful for the opportunities she had received and the experiences that had enriched her life. She was proud of her achievements, but even more so, she was proud of the person she had become-

someone who never settled for less than her best.

Savi's story became an inspiration to those around her. She encouraged others to strive for excellence, to never settle for mediocrity, and to always select the best things in life. Her unwavering belief in the pursuit of excellence had not only brought her success, but it had also enriched her life with meaning and purpose. Savi's story was a testament to the power of determination, hard work, and a commitment to always striving for the best.

How can you maintain your strong mindset?

- Always select the best things in your life.

- Never compromise with the quality of anything.

- Always strive for your excellence.

- Never settle for mediocrity.

- Give your 100% efforts whatever you do in your life.

- Be committed to excellence.

- Develop your talents and skills.

- Improve yourself every day.

- Be dedicated in your work.

- Nurture the meaningful relationships with everyone.

- Surround yourself with the positive people.

• Avoid the negative people and the negative environment.

• Build a supportive network with your loved ones.

• Never lose the sight of your belief in selecting the best things in your life.

• See the obstacles as your golden opportunities.

• Learn and grow every day.

~***~

"The most important relationship in your life is the relationship you have with yourself. Because no matter what happens, you will always be with yourself."

---Diane Von Furstenberg

Chapter 8

Be your own best friend

Be your own best friend.

Figure out your best friend inside you.

Only you can help yourself like your best friend.

Only you can guide yourself like your best friend.

Never feel alone in your life.

You're not alone, because your thoughts are with you.

Your thoughts are your best friends.

They can change your mind.

Never feel alone in your life.

You're not alone, because your conscience is with you.

Your conscience is your best friend.

It always guides you.

Never feel alone in your life.

You're not alone, because your wisdom is with you.

Your wisdom is your best friend.

It always teaches you.

Never feel alone in your life.

You're not alone, because your knowledge is with you.

Your knowledge is your best friend.

It always shows you a new direction.

Never feel alone in your life.

You're not alone, because your intuition is with you.

Your intuition is your best friend.

It always helps you to realize yourself.

~***~

Always find your best friend inside you.

If you do good deeds for yourself, you'll become your own best friend.

If you do bad deeds for yourself, you'll become your own worst enemy.

You can make friendship as well as enmity with yourself.

Make friendship with yourself.

You, yourself is the best person to make a friendship.

Always find your best friend inside you.

If you do good deeds for yourself, you'll become your own best friend.

~***~

Once upon a time, in a bustling town nestled among rolling green hills, there lived a young girl named Anupama. She was a kind and compassionate soul, but she often found herself feeling lonely and unsure of herself. Anupama had many friends, but she often struggled with self-doubt and relied heavily on others for validation.

One day, while taking a solitary walk along a winding path that led to a serene meadow, Anupama stumbled upon a talking owl named Pawan. She was initially surprised but soon realized that Pawan was no ordinary owl. He was wise and had a gentle and soothing voice that instantly put Anupama at ease.

Pawan sensed Anupama's inner turmoil and offered her some advice. "Anupama, my dear, the most important friendship you can cultivate is the one with yourself. Be your own best friend." He said with a twinkle in his eye.

Anupama was intrigued and asked Pawan how she could do that. Pawan explained that being your own best friend means treating yourself with the same kindness, love, and respect that you would offer to your dearest friend. It means valuing yourself, believing in yourself, and taking care of your well-being.

Anupama took Pawan's words to heart and embarked on a journey of self-discovery. She learned to listen to her own inner voice, to acknowledge her strengths and weaknesses without judgment, and to celebrate her accomplishments, no matter how small. She discovered her passions and pursued them with confidence and determination.

Whenever Anupama faced challenges or setbacks, she turned to her newfound friendship with herself for comfort and guidance. She learned to offer herself words of encouragement, to be patient and forgiving with herself, and to trust her own instincts. She realized that she didn't need constant validation from others because she had her own unwavering support.

As Anupama grew, she noticed a remarkable change in her life. She felt more content and fulfilled, and her relationships with others improved. She no longer sought external validation or felt the need to conform to others' expectations. Instead, she lived authentically, true to herself, and made choices that aligned with her values and beliefs.

One day, while sitting by a tranquil pond, reflecting on her journey, Anupama realized that she had become her own best friend. She had cultivated a deep sense of self-love and acceptance, and it radiated from within her. She was no longer lonely because she had herself as a constant companion, guiding her with unwavering support and love.

Anupama continued to cherish her friendship with Pawan, the wise owl, who had been her guiding light on her path to self-discovery. She thanked him for his invaluable wisdom and bid him farewell, knowing that she had found a treasure that would stay with her forever- the gift of being her own best friend. She smiled as she looked ahead to the bright future that awaited her, knowing that she was now equipped to face any challenge with confidence and grace, armed with the most powerful friendship of all- the one with herself. And so, Anupama's story became a testament to

the beautiful and fulfilling journey of being your
own best friend.

69

How can you maintain your strong mindset?

- Love yourself.

- Be kind and compassionate.

- Never feel lonely.

- Be your own best friend.

- Give up your self-doubts and negativities.

- Don't rely on others for validation.

- Cultivate friendship with yourself.

- Treat yourself with the same kindness, love, and respect that you offer to your dearest friend.

- Value yourself.

- Believe in yourself.

- Take care of your own well-being.

- Learn to discover yourself.

• Listen to your own inner-voice.

• Acknowledge your own strengths and weaknesses without judgment.

• Celebrate your own accomplishments, no matter how small.

• Discover your own passions and pursue them with confidence and determination.

• Whenever you face challenges or setbacks, turn to your newfound friendship with yourself for comfort and guidance.

• Learn to offer yourself the words of encouragement.

• Be patient.

• Forgive yourself.

• Trust your own instincts.

"Our environment, the world in which we live and work, is a mirror of our attitudes and expectations."

---Earl Nightingale

Chapter 9

Build a healthy environment around you

Build a healthy environment around you.

You'll grow and develop yourself the way your environment is.

Your mind, body and soul all are influenced by the environment where you live.

If you're living in the positive environment,

You will automatically become positive.

If you're living in the negative environment,

You will automatically become negative.

If you're living in the healthy environment,

You will automatically become healthy.

If you're living in the unhealthy environment,

You will automatically become unhealthy.

Only you can build your healthy environment around you.

You're the builder of your own healthy environment.

You're responsible for your own environment.

If you want to bring happiness, peace and tranquility in your life, then build the healthy environment around you.

Only you can build your healthy environment around you.

~***~

Once upon a time, in a bustling city filled with noise, pollution, and stress, there was a young man named Amit. Amit was tired of the negativity and chaos that surrounded him, and he decided to take matters into his own hands by building a positive environment around him.

Amit started by focusing on his own mindset. He realized that in order to create a positive environment, he needed to start from within. He practiced mindfulness and self-reflection, learning to manage his thoughts and emotions in a healthy way. He cultivated a positive attitude and made a conscious effort to see the good in every situation.

Next, Amit turned his attention to his immediate surroundings. He decided to create a sanctuary of positivity in his home. He decluttered his space, filled it with plants, and decorated it with uplifting quotes and artwork. He made his home a place of peace and serenity, where he could recharge and rejuvenate.

Amit also sought out like-minded individuals who shared his values. He joined clubs and groups that aligned with his interests, such as volunteering, outdoor activities, and personal development. He surrounded himself with positive and supportive people who encouraged and inspired him.

One day, Amit had a brilliant idea to spread positivity beyond his immediate circle. He decided to start a community garden in a vacant lot near his apartment. He enlisted the help of his neighbors and organized regular gardening sessions. The community garden quickly became a place where people could come together, connect with nature, and enjoy the fruits of their labor.

As the community garden grew, so did the positive ripple effects. The once-neglected lot transformed into a lush and vibrant green space, attracting attention from passerby. People started stopping by to admire the flowers, chat with the gardeners, and even join in the gardening activities. The community garden became a symbol of hope, resilience, and collaboration in the neighborhood.

Inspired by the success of the community garden, Amit decided to take his positive initiatives to the workplace. He started a "Gratitude and Appreciation" campaign at his office, encouraging his colleagues to express gratitude and show appreciation for each other's work. He also organized team-building activities that focused on collaboration, communication, and positive reinforcement.

As time went on, Amit's positive environment began to spread beyond his immediate community. His neighbors, colleagues, and friends were inspired by his actions and started their own positive initiatives. The community garden became a model for other neighborhoods, and his workplace became known for its supportive and uplifting culture.

Amit's efforts did not go unnoticed. He received recognition for his contributions to the community and was invited to share his story at local events and workshops. He also became a mentor to others who wanted to create positive environments in their own communities.

In times, Amit's vision of a positive environment became a reality. The city that was once filled with negativity and chaos started to transform into a more uplifting and harmonious place. People began to treat each other with kindness and respect, and the sense of community and collaboration grew stronger.

Amit's journey taught him that building a positive environment starts with one person, but its impact can spread far and wide. He realized that by cultivating a positive mindset, surrounding himself with supportive people, and taking action in his community, he could make a difference in the world. He felt fulfilled knowing that he had created a positive environment around him, and he continued to inspire others to do the same.

And so, Amit's story became a testament to the power of one person's actions in building a positive environment, and it inspired others to follow in his footsteps. His city, once a chaotic place, was now a thriving community of positivity, thanks to Amit's unwavering commitment to creating a better world.

~***~

How can you maintain your strong mindset?

• Avoid the positive environment.

• Surround yourself with the positive environment.

• Build your own positive environment.

• Focus on your own positive mindset.

• Cultivate a positive attitude.

• You have to initiate yourself.

• Everything starts from within you.

• Practice mindfulness and self-reflection.

• Learn to manage your own thoughts and emotions in a healthy way.

• Make a conscious effort to see the good in every situation.

• You can make a difference in your own life.

~***~

"Stop comparing yourself to other people; you are an original. We are all different and it's okay."

---Joyce Meyer

Chapter 10

Stop comparing yourself to others

Stop comparing yourself to others.

Be happy and content with yourself.

You're the best of yourself.

You're unique in this entire world.

Love yourself.

You're complete in yourself.

Look inside yourself; you'll know your true-self.

If you compare yourself to others that means you're discouraging yourself.

You're neglecting yourself.

You're playing a game of hatred with yourself.

You're living your life with the perspectives of other people.

You're looking happiness and contentment in the lives of other people.

You're forgetting your true potentials of your life.

You're forgetting your responsibility of your life.

If you always compare yourself to others, then you'll never discover your true happiness and contentment in your entire life.

You'll always find yourself as a failure in your life.

You'll never enjoy your life fully.

If you really want to enjoy your life fully, then stop comparing yourself to others.

If you always compare yourself to others, then you'll never discover your

true happiness and contentment in your entire life.

~***~

Anecdote:

Once upon a time in a quaint village nestled among rolling hills, there was a young girl named Mahima. Mahima was a talented artist who loved to paint and create beautiful artwork. She spent hours each day in her small studio, bringing her imagination to life on the canvas.

However, Mahima had a tendency to compare herself to others. She would often look at the artwork of her fellow villagers and feel envious of their talent and success. She would question her own abilities and doubt her own worth as an artist. This constant comparison made her feel anxious and discouraged, and it dampened her creative spirit.

One day, as Mahima was taking a walk in the forest for some fresh air and inspiration, she came across a wise man. The wise man noticed Mahima's melancholic expression and asked her what was troubling her. Mahima poured her heart out, expressing her feelings of inadequacy and self-doubt.

The wise man listened patiently and then spoke with a gentle voice, "My dear Mahima, comparing yourself to others is like comparing apples to oranges. Each one has its unique flavor and sweetness. You are a talented artist with your own distinct style and voice. Embrace your uniqueness and let go of the need to compare yourself to others."

Mahima pondered on the wise man's words and realized the truth in them. She realized that her art was a reflection of her own experiences, emotions, and creativity, and it was not meant to be compared to anyone else's. She decided to take the wise man's advice and let go of the habit of comparison.

Mahima returned to her studio with a renewed sense of purpose and passion. She began to create art from a place of joy and authenticity, without worrying about what others were doing. She experimented with different styles, colors, and techniques, and allowed herself to express her true-self without fear of judgment.

As Mahima immersed herself in her art without the burden of comparison, she found herself enjoying the process more and more. She began to appreciate her own unique perspective and artistic voice. Her artwork started to stand out and gain recognition among the villages for its originality and beauty.

One day, a famous art critic visited the village to judge an art competition. Many artists from the village submitted their artwork, including Mahima. The competition was fierce, with stunning pieces from various artists. But when the winner was announced, it was Mahima's artwork that had won the first prize.

Mahima was overjoyed, not because she had won, but because she had learned the value of not comparing herself to others. She realized that her true worth as an artist came from within, and that her uniqueness was her greatest asset. She thanked the wise man for the invaluable lesson and continued to create art with joy and authenticity.

Word of Mahima's success spread beyond the village, and she began to receive invitations to exhibit her artwork in galleries in other towns and cities. Her artwork became highly sought after, and she gained a loyal following of admirers. Mahima's journey as an artist was not without challenges, but she never fell into the trap of comparison again. She continued to stay true to herself and create art that came from her heart.

Mahima's story became an inspiration to many artists and individuals alike. She learned that comparing oneself to others only leads to self-doubt and unhappiness, and that true success comes from embracing one's uniqueness and staying authentic to oneself. Mahima's art and her story touched the hearts of people far and wide, and she continued to create beautiful artwork that brought joy to many for years to come.

∼***∽

How can you maintain your strong mindset?

- Never ever compare yourself to others.

- Don't look at the works of the other people.

- Don't worry about what others are doing.

- Have faith in yourself.

- Believe in your own talents and skills.

- Don't feel envious of other's talent and success.

- Don't raise a question mark on your own abilities.

- Don't doubt on your own worth and potentials.

- Just focus on your own goal.

- Persevere with confidence and determination.

- You are unique in this entire world.

• Embrace your uniqueness.

• What you can do, nobody can do like you.

• Give up the bad habit of comparison.

• Express your true-self without fear of judgment.

• Learn to enjoy yourself in your own work.

• Appreciate your own unique perspectives of life.

• Always remember that comparing yourself to others only leads to self-doubt and unhappiness.

"Worrying doesn't take away tomorrow's troubles; it takes away today's peace."

---Randy Armstrong

Chapter 11

Forget your worries and tensions

Worries and tensions are the biggest enemies of your happiness, peace and prosperity.

Your worries and tensions are like poison that kills you every moment.

Your worries and tensions are like rust that wear out your skills and talents.

Your worries and tensions always bring unhappiness, disturbances and stresses in your life.

Your worries will only steal your happiness and contentment.

You'll become like a prisoner of your worries and tensions.

Your worries and tensions will make you weak and sick.

You'll lose your self-believe and self-confidence.

You'll become negative.

You'll become pessimistic.

Everything appears dark in front of you.

You'll see failure in every opportunity.

You'll miss the beauty of life.

You'll miss the most memorable moment of your life.

Your worries and tensions will kill you before your ultimate death.

Your worries and tensions will create confusion in your life.

Replace your worries and tensions with wise thoughts and nice planning.

Worries and tensions are your own by-products.

You yourself manufacture your own worries and tensions.

Your worries and tensions are like the heavy loads laden on your head.

The more you carry the heavy loads of your worries and tensions on you, the more you'll dump yourself inside it.

Free your mind and soul from the loads of worries and tensions

Nobody can free you from your worries and tensions.

Only you can free yourself from the web of your worries and tensions.

Figure out the root causes of your worries and tensions before it will swallow you completely.

You can't solve your problems with worries and tensions.

You can only wipe out your worries and tensions with your positive mindsets, self-believe, self-confidence and self-reliance.

If you want to witness the glorious moment in your life, then forget your worries and tensions.

If you want to glimpse happiness, peace and prosperity in your life, then forget your worries and tensions.

The more you carry the heavy loads of your worries and tensions on you, the more you'll dump yourself inside it.

~***~

Anecdote:

Once upon a time, in a small village nestled amidst rolling hills and lush greenery, there lived a young girl named Meena. Meena was known for her cheerful demeanor and her ability to find joy in the simplest of things. She was loved by everyone in the village for her kind heart and infectious laughter.

One day, Meena woke up feeling overwhelmed with worries and tensions. Her mind was clouded with thoughts of impending exams, chores that needed to be done, and responsibilities that seemed too heavy to bear. She tried to shake off the negativity by going about her daily routine, but her worries kept gnawing at her, making her lose her usual sparkle.

As Meena walked through the village square, she noticed an elderly woman sitting by a serene pond. The woman had a serene smile on her face, and she radiated a sense of tranquility that immediately caught Meena's attention. Curious, Meena approached the woman and asked her how she managed to look so calm and peaceful.

The woman introduced herself as Granny Shanti, and she had a reputation in the village for being wise and offering sage advice. She patted the spot next to her and gestured for

Meena to sit down. Meena obliged eager to learn from Granny Shanti's wisdom.

Ganny Shanti looked at Meena with kind eyes and said, "Child, worries and tensions are a part of life, but it's up to us how we choose to deal with them. Sometimes, we get so caught up in our thoughts that we forget to appreciate the present moment."

Meena nodded, realizing that she had been dwelling too much on her worries and not living in the present. Granny Shanti then shared a simple technique with Meena. She told her to closed her eyes, take a deep breath, and imagine a beautiful meadow filled with wildflowers swaying in the breeze.

Meena followed Ganny Shanti's instructions and closed her eyes, taking a deep breath. She imagined herself in the meadow, surrounded by the vibrant colors and fragrant scents of the flowers. She could feel the warmth of the sun on her skin and hear the gentle rustling of the leaves in the trees. For a moment, she forgot all her worries and tensions, and her mind felt clear and at peace.

When Meena opened her eyes, she felt a renewed sense of energy and a lighter heart. She thanked Granny Shanti and promised to practice the technique whenever she felt overwhelmed. Granny Shanti smiled and said, "Remember, child, it's important to take breaks from worrying and allow yourself to be present in the moment. Life is meant to be enjoyed."

Meena left Granny Shanti's side with a newfound sense of appreciation for the present moment. She went about her day with a lighter step and a brighter smile. She tackled her exams and chores with renewed focus and determination, but she also made sure to take breaks and immerse herself in the beauty of nature.

With time, Meena became known once again for her cheerful demeanor and zest for life. She learned to let go of worries and tensions that were beyond her control and focused on making the most of each moment. She shared Granny Shanti's wisdom with her friends and family, spreading the message of forgetting worries and tensions to live a more joyful and fulfilling life.

As years passed, Meena grew up to be a wise and contented woman, carrying the lessons she had learned from Granny Shanti with her wherever she went. She cherished the memories of that chance encounter by the pond and remained grateful for the simple yet powerful technique that had helped her forget her worries and tensions, and embrace the beauty of the present moment. And she lived happily ever after, inspiring others to do the same.

~***~

How can you maintain your strong mindset?

• Worries and tensions are the parts of your life.

• Always keep your cheerful demeanor.

• Keep your smile and laughter on your face.

• Find joy in the simplest of things.

• Be kind hearted and compassionate.

• Don't allow worries and tensions to overshadow your mind.

• Boost up your mind with positive attitude and positive outlook.

• Replace your worries and tensions with your joy, happiness, hope and patience.

• Conquer your negative thoughts with your positive thoughts.

• Manage yourself to remain calm and peaceful.

• Don't live your life in your past.

• Don't worry too much about your future.

• Live in your present moment and appreciate it.

• Always remember that life is meant to be enjoyed.

~***~

"Do not dwell in the past; do not dream of the future, concentrate the mind on the present moment."

---Lord Buddha

Chapter 12

Concentrate on your present moment

Concentrate on your present moment.

Forget your past.

Don't recall your past.

Your past is already gone.

You can't get anything from your past.

You can only learn good lessons from your past.

If you recall your past, then you can't live your life in your present moment.

You can't move ahead in your life.

Your life doesn't depend upon your past, but your life depends upon your present moment.

Whatever you do today, it will bear fruitful results in the coming days or in the coming weeks or in the coming months or in the coming years.

Your present moment is the builder of your future.

Your present is the mother of your future.

Your future depends on your present moment.

Make your present moment successful if you want to see yourself successful in your future.

Enjoy your present moment with full heart and soul.

Bury your past and reincarnate yourself.

Don't look back to your past.

Start a new journey of your life and move forward.

~***~

Anecdote:

In a bustling city, there lived a young man named Anmol. Anmol was a hardworking professional who was always on the go. He was constantly multitasking, juggling work, personal commitments, and social obligations. He was known for his ambition and determination, but he often found himself feeling stressed and overwhelmed.

One day, as Anmol was rushing to a meeting, he bumped into an old man on the street. The old man had a serene expression on his face, and he radiated a sense of calmness that intrigued Anmol. The old man introduced himself as Mr. Chandra and asked Anmol why he seemed so flustered.

Anmol shared his concerns with Mr. Chandra, expressing how he was always thinking about the future, worrying about deadlines, and feeling anxious about upcoming events. Mr. Chandra listened patiently and then offered Anmol a simple piece of advice: "Son, learn to concentrate on your present moment."

At first, Anmol was puzzled. He had always been taught to plan for the future and work towards his goals. However, something about Mr. Chandra's words resonated with him, and he decided to give it a try.

The next day, Anmol woke up with a fresh mindset. Instead of rushing through his day, he decided to be fully present in each moment. When he was at work, he focused on his tasks without worrying about what was coming up next. When he was spending time with his friends and family, he put away his phone and truly engaged in conversations.

Anmol also started practicing mindfulness, taking moments throughout the day to be aware of his thoughts, feelings, and sensations without judgment. He noticed the beauty in simple things, like the taste of his morning coffee or the warmth of the sun on his face during a lunchtime walk.

As days turned into weeks, Anmol found that he felt less stressed and more fulfilled. He was able to work more efficiently and enjoy his time with loved ones without distractions. He realized that by concentrating on his present moment, he was able to fully experience life and appreciate the joys that were right in front of him.

One day, Anmol received an unexpected promotion at work. While he was thrilled about the news, he realized that he had been so caught up in his worries about the future that he had forgotten to celebrate his accomplishments along the way. He decided to take Mr. Chandra out for a cup of tea to express his gratitude and share how his life had changed.

When Anmol met Mr. Chandra, he noticed that the old man still the same serene expression on his face. Anmol thanked him for his wise advice and shared how he had learned to concentrate on his present moment. Mr. Chandra smiled and said, "Son, life is a series of moments, and it's up to us to make the most of them. The present moment is all we have, so why not embrace it fully?"

Anmol nodded, realized the profound wisdom in Mr. Chandra's words. He thanked him once again and bid him farewell, feeling grateful for the encounter that had changed his life.

From that day on, Anmol continued to practice being present in each moment. He learned to let go of worries about the future and regrets about the past, and instead, he focused on making the most of the present. He found joy in the simple pleasures of life and cultivated meaningful connections with others.

With time, Anmol achieved success in his career, but he also learned to appreciate the journey rather than just the destination. He lived a more balanced and fulfilling life, cherishing each moment as it came, and inspiring others to do the same. And he lived happily, fully immersed in the beauty of the present moment.

~***~

How can you maintain your strong mindset?

• Don't get stressed in your life.

• Your stress is the root cause of your anxieties and depressions.

• Be easy in your approach.

• Don't get hurried.

• Learn to pause for a moment in your life.

• Stop over thinking about your future.

• Concentrate on your present moment.

• Don't regret about your past deeds and experiences.

• Focus on your tasks without worrying about what is coming up next.

• Cultivate the meaningful connections with others.

- Be social with your loved ones, friends and colleagues.

- Do meditation, yoga and exercise every day.

- Be aware of your own thoughts, feelings and sensations without judgment.

- Don't entangle yourself in the complex things in your life.

- Live a simple living and high thinking formula in your life.

- Experience your life fully and appreciate the joys that are right in front of you.

- Don't forget to celebrate your small accomplishments.

- Embrace your present moment fully.

- Live a balanced life and fulfilling life and cherish each moment as it comes.

- Immerse yourself in the beauty of your present moment.

~***~

About the author:

Birister Sharma is a full time author. He is also an avid reader. He loves reading, writing, and motivation. He has penned down dozens of self-help motivational books and novels so far.

You may contact him @ birister2007@gmail.com